NEW VANGUARD 207

MEDIUM MARK A WHIPPET

DAVID FLETCHER   ILLUSTRATED BY HENRY MORESHEAD

First published in Great Britain in 2014 by Osprey Publishing,
PO Box 883, Oxford, OX1 9PL, UK
PO Box 3985, New York, NY 10185-3985, USA
E-mail: info@ospreypublishing.com

Osprey Publishing is part of the Osprey Group

A CIP catalogue record for this book is available from the British Library

Print ISBN: 978 1 78200 398 4
PDF ebook ISBN: 978 1 78200 399 1
ePub ebook ISBN: 978 1 78200 400 4

Index by Alan Thatcher
Typeset in Sabon and Myriad Pro
Originated by PDQ Media, Bungay, UK
Printed in China through Worldprint Ltd

14 15 16 17 18 10 9 8 7 6 5 4 3 2 1

Osprey Publishing is supporting the Woodland Trust, the UK's leading
woodland conservation charity, by funding the dedication of trees.

www.ospreypublishing.com

CONTENTS

MEDIUM MARK A WHIPPET

THE WHIPPET'S FORERUNNER: THE TRITTON CHASER

According to the engineer William Tritton, credited as one of the inventors of the tank, he was asked to produce a lighter tank when he visited the Somme on 20 September 1916. This was only five days since tanks had been launched onto the battlefield for the very first time. Tritton does not say who requested this, but the implication must be that it was Sir Douglas Haig, Commander-in-Chief of the British Expeditionary Force (BEF), either directly or through his staff. No matter who was responsible, it was either remarkably prescient or a very lucky guess. It is valid to ask whether the idea of a faster, lighter machine was considered as an alternative to the slower, heavier tanks, or as an adjunct to them, which we have always assumed, but the fact that Tritton's design did not have the trench crossing ability of the heavy tanks, and that improved versions of the heavy tank were developed, must support the adjunct theory in retrospect.

It is interesting to consider what fellow engineer Walter Wilson, another crucial contributor to the early tank, knew of all this. Given his close association with Tritton, and the fact that he was later appointed joint Director of Design for the Mechanical Warfare Department, it seems unlikely that he was entirely ignorant of developments. In a paper that appears to be dated towards the end of 1916, he speculates on future developments, including that of a light tank that, he says, would need only lowslung tracks and perhaps a turret. All of this suggests that he knew full well that Tritton was working on a lighter model, yet he says nothing at all about the driving system or transmission, which is odd bearing in mind that these were his areas of expertise. Perhaps he knew what Tritton was planning but elected to keep his opinions to himself. However, he also seemed to be aware of what Harry Ricardo, another engineer, was doing in terms of designing a more powerful engine for the heavy tanks, and implies, although he does not actually say so, that this engine would also be very effective in a lighter type of tank.

The story of the invention of the tank published by William Foster & Co shortly after World War I, *The Tank: Its Birth and Development*, while largely company propaganda, is remarkably specific about dates. It states, for example, that design work on Tritton's light machine, later to be known as the 'Whippet', commenced on 10 November 1916, and that construction began on 21 December the same year. It has been said that Tritton based his design on the prototype machine 'Little Willie' (see NVG100), but there is no

hard evidence for this beyond the low profile of the track frames. Even so, this may explain a comment in an old Tank Museum publication that claims that Tritton first designed a light tank in 1915.

Foster's claim that the prototype was able to move itself by 3 February 1917 and embarked upon its first trial eight days later suggests that it was effectively complete, but the date that stands out in the Whippet's history must be 3 March 1917. On that day the Ministry of Munitions staged a demonstration of experimental tanks on a testing ground at Oldbury near Birmingham. Ostensibly arranged to try out a selection of experimental transmission systems in heavy tank hulls, the opportunity was also taken to introduce two experimental prototypes, the original Gun Carrier machine and what was now described as the 'Tritton Chaser'.

The programme that accompanied the event included a simple drawing of each tank and a reasonably detailed technical description, but the drawing of the Tritton Chaser has always been controversial. It shows the tank fitted with a small rotating turret, which, according to the description, contained a single Lewis gun. However, since every known photograph of the tank shows it with the more familiar angled superstructure, it has been claimed that the drawing was an early concept that had been changed before it was completed. Alas for such logical speculation, two photographs showing

The Whippet as first built with the offset rotating turret. Notice the socket for an engine starting handle and the very limited vision slit for the driver. At this stage the tank also had its fuel tank at the back, resulting in the square front end. Notice that a name, 'The Whippet', has also been painted on the front end of the tank.

the machine with a turret, as in the drawing, subsequently surfaced, so there is no longer any need to speculate.

Although it is described as the Tritton Chaser in the programme, the caption beneath the drawing tells us that it is Tritton's Light Machine No. 2 (EMB). The names were interchangeable, although the former was more appealing. 'Number 2' was simply the tank's place in the display and should not be taken to suggest that it was Tritton's second design, while 'EMB' gives its official designation of 'Experimental Machine B', a system which appears to have been applied on an inconsistent basis. To make absolutely sure that the various tank models could readily be identified, each one (except for the gun carrying machine) was painted in a distinguishing colour. Exactly how this was done is again not entirely clear, but such evidence as there is suggests that it took the form of a broad stripe running around the hull about midway up. For the Tritton Chase, the distinguishing colour was green.

Since it is clear from the illustrations, there is no need to describe the outward appearance of the machine, but there are various notes in the Oldbury programme that might be expanded upon. The Tritton Chaser is introduced as an attempt to meet the requirements of the military authorities for a light machine capable of maintaining higher speeds than the standard type. So speed was the primary issue, suggesting perhaps a form of tracked armoured car. The paragraph ends with the simple sentence 'Its twin engine transmission is worthy of note'. It is also clear from the Oldbury programme that at this time it was turreted, since under 'Armament' it states 'the armament consists of one Lewis gun in a gun turret'.

The mechanical arrangements of the Chaser are shown in the programme drawing and, since they are the same as in the production Whippet, can be treated here in some detail. At the front was a pair of 7,720cc Tylor JB4

A

1: TRITTON'S CHASER 'THE WHIPPET' IN ORIGINAL FORM.

William Tritton was encouraged to design a faster light tank when he visited the Somme on 20 September 1916, and the finished tank was ready to take part in the Oldbury Trials of 3 March 1917 in a suburb of Birmingham. The new tank was quite distinctive, with low-profile track frames, a small cylindrical turret on the left with a driver's cab alongside on the right. A green stripe was painted around the tank for identification purposes for the benefit of those attending the trial.

In its original form the Chaser was a two-man tank with a driver on the right and the gunner/commander in the rotating turret on the left, which was intended to carry a single .303-inch Lewis machine gun. It was driven by a pair of Tylor 45hp engines and was always a difficult tank to drive. With a top speed of over 8mph it was effectively twice as fast as a contemporary heavy tank and every bit as manoeuvrable, but it did not have a heavy tank's impressive trench-crossing capability.

2: THE TRITTON CHASER REBUILT

Subsequently William Tritton's prototype Chaser tank was rebuilt and modified on a number of occasions until it looked more like the production machines, although it retained a full set of Skefco roller bearings on each side. The most significant change was the removal of the rotating turret and its replacement by an angular, fixed superstructure with a door at the back and possible mounting places for Hotchkiss machine guns on all four faces. Another important change was the transfer of the 70-gallon petrol tank from a location at the back, between the rear tracks, to a position on the nose.

The tank latterly spent a lot of its time at the Mechanical Warfare Department's Experimental Station at Dollis Hill, North London, where it was photographed on a number of occasions – once equipped with a modified version of the wheeled tail device as fitted to the early Mark I tanks. The tank spent its final days, after the war, as an exhibit in the original Imperial War Museum collection in the grounds of the Crystal Palace in Upper Norwood.

1

2

45hp, four-cylinder engines, normally running at 1,200rpm. Manufactured by the Tylor Company of King's Cross, London, they were typical of their day, with the cylinders cast in pairs, side valve and water-cooled. Single Tylor engines were fitted to the War Department's AEC Y Type 3-ton cargo trucks, and, perhaps more memorably, to late production versions of the legendary B Type double-deck bus of that era. Linked to a rugged four-speed and reverse gearbox, the engine produced a hard-wearing combination highly suited to a military vehicle, or indeed a bus.

The only modification required to get two of these engines alongside one another in a tank was that they were 'handed' i.e. the inlet and outlet valves on the left side engine were reversed so that the exhaust manifold would be situated on the outside in each case. Each engine had its own flywheel and cone clutch, behind which was its own gearbox, of the conventional type rather than the multi-chain version originally used on the B Type bus.

From the driver's point of view, the Whippet must have been something of a nightmare. In his seat, offset to the right of the turret, he was faced with a steering wheel, which also supported the ignition controls, two complete sets of gear controls and clutch pedals to go with them, and two handbrake levers.

There was no differential in the usual sense. Each engine and gearbox drove its own track through a 90° worm drive onto a divided half shaft, from the outer ends of which a sprocket and chain arrangement translated drive to the rear mounted track drive sprocket on each side. There would have been occasions when one track started to slip badly, when it would have helped to have a device that linked the two half-shafts together. On the Tritton Chaser, according to the Oldbury programme, a simple dog-clutch system was employed to serve the purpose of a differential lock. In practice this may have placed too great a strain on the mechanism, because production Whippets are said to have had a limited slip clutch that became effective when the difference in power output from the two engines exceeded 12hp. This would have made driving on one engine extremely difficult, should the need ever arise, but not quite impossible.

There are certain things about the Tritton Chaser that we do not know. It seems reasonable to suppose that the radiator (or radiators) were located ahead of the engines, as they were in the production Whippets, but this remains unproven. It also seems likely that at this stage in its development the Whippet was started by a hand crank inserted at the front, via a hole in line with the port side engine, although this certainly changed later. Another change was the location of the fuel tank, which initially Tritton placed at the back of his machine, down between the track frames.

There can be no doubt why Tritton elected to use this twin engine system; it enabled one man to drive the tank, compared with four men on what was then described as a 'standard' tank. More or less the same arrangement was planned for the proposed 'super-tank' Flying Elephant, largely one imagines in pursuit of more power, although it may also have been part of the steering arrangements. One could speculate at length upon why Tritton does not appear to have consulted his colleague Walter Wilson on this, and indeed why Wilson does not appear to have been involved in the design of the Chaser at all. Tritton was a businessman as well as an engineer, so it makes sense that he would look for something simple and robust that could be assembled from available components rather than anything that might be pushing the limits of technology. He may also have felt that, while helping his country and the war effort, it would do no harm to have a design of his own that might one day have some commercial application, should it prove successful.

The greatest difficulty we have is in pinpointing the date when the Tritton Chaser changed shape and was rebuilt without the turret. It seems safe to assume that in its original, turreted form the tank had a crew of two; the over-worked driver and the gunner/commander squeezed into his little turret. Perhaps it was simply that problems of communication between the two rendered the tank unfightable. All we can say for sure is that the tank was turreted when it took part in the Oldbury trials, but was probably converted not long afterwards, as the tank was seen at a similar event with a rigid, angular superstructure instead of the rotating turret and, at a later time still, it was photographed with the fuel tank relocated to the front. This may well have been connected to the problem of centre of gravity. Concerns had already been expressed about the tendency of designers to add features and, as a consequence, weight to the rear of vehicles, which had a serious adverse effect upon the centre of gravity.

The Whippet prototype photographed at Dollis Hill towing a Mark IV. It is easily identified by having roller bearings at all wheel stations, but notice also the fuel tank, moved to the front but rounded on top. The Mark IV seems to be being towed as a deadweight load, perhaps to test the hauling powers of the lighter tank.

In this form, with certain detail differences, the tank was near enough identical to a production Whippet, although the prototype would have been constructed from unarmoured steel, which was easier to work. In order to achieve all-round fire, machine-gun mountings were now provided in all four faces of the superstructure. The superstructure, especially at the front, was extremely complicated and better illustrated than described. However, it is notable that the left side stands proud of the driver's position, totally obscuring his view in that direction, as indeed the turret did. There was now room for three, maybe even four in the cab, which relieved the commander from being the only gunner.

Since the Tritton Chaser, in its final form, is virtually indistinguishable from a production Whippet, it is useful to know that there is one certain way of telling them apart. In order to reduce rolling resistance and improve speed, Tritton fitted his Chaser with a full set of Skefco roller bearings on each side. Since there are 32 rollers (16 each side), the bearing caps are quite obvious. On production tanks, the number of rollers remained the same, but only the load-bearing six on each side were fitted with roller bearings and thus the distinctive bearing caps.

The ultimate fate of the Tritton Chaser is known. Towards the end of the war it was seen in the background of a photograph taken at the Mechanical Warfare Supply Department testing ground at Dollis Hill in north London, where it is sporting a pair of wheels on a frame at the rear similar to those seen on Mark I tanks in 1916. These had been fitted as a means of assisting the tank over wider trenches. A report issued after the war speaks of an experimental tail skid being fitted for the same purpose, but says that both attachments tended to take the weight off the tracks and reduce grip. The report goes on to say that the wheeled alternative was better in this respect, but still not good enough. When the war was over, the Tritton Chaser was included in a representative collection of tanks displayed at the original Imperial War Museum at the Crystal Palace in Upper Norwood, but was cut up for scrap when the museum transferred to a new site.

PRODUCTION OF THE WHIPPET

Foster & Co's book *The Tank: Its Birth and Development* claims that a total of 400 Whippets were ordered. However, only 200 were ever completed. These were the tanks built by William Foster & Co, which were numbered A200 to A399. It was normal practice not to begin each group of tanks from 1, since it immediately gave the enemy an indication of how many tanks of each type had been produced. However, it does raise the question of why the prefix A was used.

The same arrangement was employed with the gun carrier machines, which were numbered from GC100 onwards. However, since neither of these groups of numbers clashed with any other used for tanks, this form of categorization cannot have been for that reason. It was not used on subsequent models, the Medium B or Medium C. Perhaps it was instituted in order to make it clear that medium tanks were to be categorized in an alphabetical sequence instead of a numerical one, but that does not explain why it was dropped afterwards. All 200 of the Medium A Whippets were assembled at the Wellington Foundry in Lincoln, but photographs taken

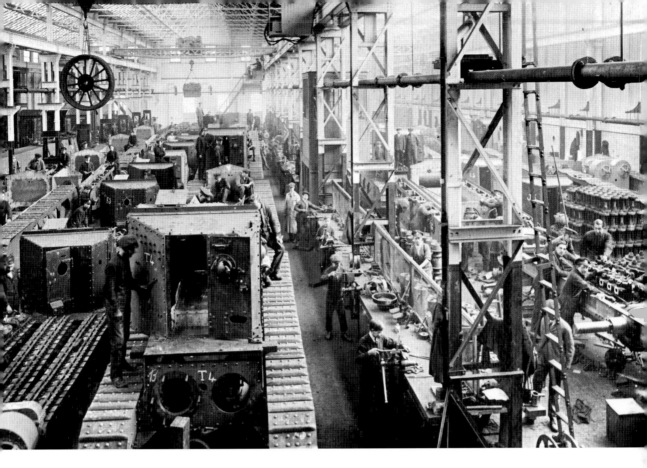

of the assembly lines show what appears to be a slightly haphazard arrangement. Tanks on the extreme left are little more than chassis, while those on the centre line are more complete and those on the right are even less advanced. Even so, once they were completed, the tanks were taken out onto some rough ground adjacent to the plant and put through their paces.

Although most of their significant features and crew duties are described elsewhere, there are others that warrant examination. For example, the location of the engines, under armoured covers at the front, was not accessible from inside the tank. Despite a large opening in the front of the cab that meant that they were visible, any maintenance carried out could be done only by the crew's dismounting, going to the front, and lifting the armoured cover over the engine. Any work that had to be done required at least one man to work in the open, vulnerable to any fire that might have been flying about. On a heavy tank, by contrast, the location of the engine within the body of the tank meant that repair work could be carried out under the protection of the tank's armour.

It would be wrong to suppose that all 200 tanks were built at around the same time. Production was steady, but it was the summer of 1918 before the majority, 166 tanks, were actually completed, and a further three months before the rest appeared. Thus, although there were more than enough tanks, only two battalions were ever completed with the new tanks. There are rumours of a further 200 tanks being ordered in the summer of 1917, but it is unclear from whom. For a while, 400 Whippets were theoretically on order before being cancelled about four months later. It is not entirely clear why this order was revoked, since two heavy tank battalions were

An interior view of Foster's works, the Wellington Foundry, showing Whippets under construction. The purpose of the wheel, hanging from the overhead crane, is not clear. Everything is on show here, from incomplete chassis to nearly finished tanks.

New Whippets being tested on waste land outside Foster's factory in Lincoln. There is also a Mark IV in the picture, although Whippets are clearly the focus of attention. The driving course seems to include different levels of ground in order to test each tank's cross-country ability.

obliged to operate Mark IV tanks right through to the end of the war. The battalions could certainly have used the Whippets and it is known that some of the later formations, such as the 17th, were originally earmarked for completion as Whippet battalions.

None of this seems to have been understood or appreciated by General Headquarters (GHQ) in France. Almost immediately after the Oldbury demonstration, Sir Douglas Haig is reported to have asked for 200 of the new tanks to be delivered in France by the end of July 1917. Since the tank demonstrated at Oldbury was only a prototype and even then not in its final form, the size of this order would appear to be very optimistic to the point of being ridiculous. On the other hand, it does suggest that the staff at GHQ appreciated the potential of the new tank, even if they rather underestimated the degree of work involved in producing it.

DRIVING THE WHIPPET

Among the crew of a Whippet, the only man who had a seat was the driver. Behind him was a rack of ammunition boxes and ahead of him the controls. On the bulkhead in front of him was the visor through which he viewed the way ahead, and high up on the front wall was the Autovac fuel feed system. Directly in front of him was a steering wheel, which also incorporated the ignition control. The wheel was linked to both engine throttles so that the engines could be used to steer the tank. This was described in the driver's handbook as very 'light', which is taken to mean responsive, but it had its limits. This method of steering would not work when both engines were running at maximum power or when both had been throttled back to minimum revolutions, because the two throttles needed a bit of leeway to play with.

When driving at low power, below the level at which the engine governors came into effect, there was a tendency for the engines to react slightly differently to the throttle settings, causing the tank to 'hunt' or steer indiscriminately one way or the other. On normal ground this did not seem to matter very much, but in confined spaces, or for example when the tank was climbing onto a railway wagon, it was recommended that the driver engage the friction clutch, operated by a lever on the left side of his seat, which was effective so long as the difference in engine power between the two engines did not exceed 12hp.

First, however, it was necessary to start the engines using a crank handle. When it was safe to do so, the handle could be inserted from outside the tank at the back, but in action there was a secondary crank position on the inside, which required two men to turn it. The cramped conditions inside the cab made this difficult. It was also necessary for a crew member to raise a small lever at one side of the cab, which engaged the starting handle with the crankshaft of each engine while it was being started. The process was reversed when it came to starting the second engine. It was possible to start one engine if the other was already running by setting both gearboxes into reverse and driving backwards on the working engine until the other one fired up. However, this worked only on reasonably soft ground where the tracks could get a grip.

The driver had two clutch pedals and two complete gearboxes, with four forward speeds and one reverse in each. The gear change levers were located on either side of his seat, slightly forward and within easy reach of his right and left arms. The gears were changed sequentially during acceleration, not at the same time. However, since each gearbox was of the constant mesh type, it was possible to change gear while the tank was moving, something that was not possible in a heavy tank. This required the driver to double-declutch up and down each box.

The clutch pedals, integral to the working of the gearboxes, were located in front of the driver's seat. These worked in the conventional way. The initial movement detached the drive from the engine and could be used to provide a free steering capability, although this only worked on very favourable ground. A more effective method of steering was to depress the clutch pedal even further in order to engage a brake, normally the clutch stop, which would also serve as a steering brake.

Even driving in a straight line was far from easy, since gears had to be changed successively up and down the box. For example, assuming that the driver had got the tank moving in first gear, the drill for shifting up to second was to depress one clutch pedal, move the gear lever on that side to neutral, raise and depress the clutch again, shift into second and then raise the clutch. This would be repeated on the second gearbox and so on up through the range as required. Naturally a skilled driver would slip through these evolutions in no time at all, and the system had the advantage, at least over the heavy tanks, that gears could be changed on the move, so that the tank could accelerate through the range from the minimum speed in first

A new Whippet being demonstrated to the press, probably in France but well behind the lines. An officer is riding outside the cab at the back, perhaps in order to avoid being roasted alive.

An early Whippet on test, with the rear door open. Notice that it is marked 'Soft Plate', suggesting that this tank has not undergone the full armouring process. This tank also lacks a lot of the details normally seen on service Whippets, and is also deficient in machine-gun mountings.

of 1¾mph (2.8kph) to a maximum of 8mph (12.9kph) in fourth. Speed, in the world of World War I tanks, is only ever a relative term.

In order to steer, the driver had various options. One was the variable throttle control as already described, which, by turning the wheel to the left, speeded up the right-hand engine and slowed down the left. This was transmitted through to the tracks, so that the tank would start to make a gentle turn to the left. This seems to have been the preferred method, since geared steering carried with it the risk of stalling one engine in the process. It has been said that the tank could spin around in its own length by having one gearbox in a forward gear and one in reverse, but this is not advised anywhere in contemporary documents and may well have been impractical. Recommended practice when making a sharp turn, or manoeuvring in a tight space, was to disengage drive to one side, either by declutching or knocking the gear into neutral, and powering the tank round by the other track. This would be enhanced by applying a brake to the undriven track, just as in a heavy tank. An extra brake drum with an external contracting band around, it was attached to an extension of each worm shaft. Operated from two levers directly in front of the driver, these were used as parking brakes and were very powerful. The drive from each gearbox passed through a worm gear

B **ABANDONED TANKS AT BRAY SUR SOMME**

Towards the end of March 1918, when the great German offensive was at its height, 3rd Tank Brigade was at a training ground at Bray sur Somme a few miles west of Peronne, training men to drive and maintain Whippets. Five or six tanks had been laid up with engine trouble and with the Germans drawing close, and no spares available, it was decided to sabotage these tanks in order to render them useless to the enemy. By the time the men had finished many of the tanks had been pulled apart and bits were strewn everywhere.

When the Germans captured Bray sur Somme they discovered the tanks but concluded that they were all quite beyond repair and, apart from painting the claim that they had been captured on their sides, left the tanks alone. The tanks remained there until the area was recaptured some months later. The tanks were found, and photographed, just as they had been left, but what happened to them after that is not recorded. They may have been broken up for scrap, or possibly repaired for further service.

A Whippet photographed near Demuin, on active service. Notice that two members of the crew, but not the driver, are travelling outside to avoid the heat, and see also the array of spare fuel cans tied on at the front. Its machine guns do not appear to be mounted, but you can see the canvas track guards on both sides.

to a driving chain pinion shaft. From this gear, the drive passed by chain to pinions that meshed with the track drive sprockets at the rear on either side.

THE WHIPPET IN ACTION

Whippets first arrived in small numbers at the Western Front in December 1917. To begin with, only one or two were delivered to the 3rd, 6th and 9th battalions, but over the next couple of months they appeared in dribs and drabs, gradually replacing the Mark IV tanks that the battalions had used at Cambrai and earlier. Even so, the units remained Mark IV battalions for the duration, although of course no actions were fought over this period.

Whippets were issued to C Company, 9th Battalion Tank Corps in April 1918, and although often sent forward fully equipped to fight never in fact saw any combat action with the 9th. Two months later they were passed on to the 3rd Battalion and were replaced in the 9th by Mark V tanks, bringing C Company into line with the rest of the battalion. In fact for a while C Company, 9th Battalion operated with the two Whippet equipped companies of the 3rd Battalion, A and C companies (B Company was formed into Lewis gun teams at this time).

A very unusual arrangement: a Whippet being used to launch a French fishing boat at Bray Dunes. How much the driver can see of what he is doing is a bit of a puzzle. This was obviously not a normal duty for Whippets, and may be classified as help to the civilian population.

The 3rd Tank Brigade, which was in the process of converting to Whippets, was in reserve at Bray-sur-Somme, north-east of Amiens. Of its constituent battalions, only the 3rd was fit to fight, and a dozen tanks of C Company were dispatched to deal with the enemy, which was reported to be massing south-west of Cambrai. Arriving at the village of Colincamps around noon on 26 March 1918, they ran headlong into a couple of German battalions, which, seeing that tanks were upon them, broke and fled. The tanks pursued them eastwards almost to Serre and effectively broke up the momentum of the attack, killing and capturing a fair number of the attackers. This was regarded as an excellent early trial of the Whippets under combat conditions. Most of them had been running continuously for 16 hours before the action began, yet went straight into action and did not experience any mechanical failures at all. How the crews fared is not recorded. C Company, however, was commanded at this time by Captain T. R. (Tommy) Price, who about a month later would be engaged in a very similar action.

At the same time, farther south, the Germans were sweeping across the country and the tank training area at Bray-sur-Somme was in their path. Five or six Whippets allocated for driver training were undergoing repairs, and since these could not be repaired in time they had to be wrecked by Tank Corps personnel and abandoned. These were therefore captured by the advancing Germans who, unable to repair them either, could only leave them where they stood, which is exactly how they were found when the area was recaptured some six months later.

On 14 April 1918 3rd Battalion was visited by Sir William Tritton, the designer of the Whippet. He was treated to a conference at which suggestions were put forward for improvements to the tank. These are not specified, but cannot have been very many, since the only action the Whippets had been involved in up to now had been very successful. It had not involved cavalry or trenches, so one imagines that the majority of comments were confined to the unpleasant conditions inside the tank. The designer was not in a position to do much about this at the time, but the comments may have had some bearing on his later design for the Medium C tank, which was particularly good in this respect.

Five days later, on 19 April, the Whippet tanks held in brigade reserve were formed into a temporary X Company, command of which was handed to Tommy Price. On the 22nd, X Company moved up closer to the line in aposition of readiness. The enemy were attacking heavily all along the line, aiming to isolate or capture Amiens in the aftermath of their great spring

An interesting comparison: a Medium A Whippet and Renault FT-17 light tank together at Bovington Camp. Although both were classified as light or medium tanks, they were surprisingly large.

offensive, which had now been halted. It would be tempting to see the Whippets as a planned and deliberate ideal antidote to mass infantry attack, owing to their relatively greater speed and manoeuvrability, but the fact that they were in the area was the most likely reason why they were used. They simply happened to be in the right place at the right time.

On 24 April 1918, X Company was in action at Cachy. The company consisted of seven Whippet tanks: four from H Section, 3rd Battalion (the section commanded by Lieutenant L. B. Hore) and three from E Section, commanded by Lieutenant A. Elsbury, the whole company being under the command of Captain Price. Advancing into an area that appeared to be devoid of British defenders, the seven tanks ran into two battalions of enemy troops from the 77th Reserve Division advancing to attack. The tanks swept into action with their machine guns firing and effectively carved up both battalions, chasing them off the field and claiming about 400 dead. However, four Whippets were hit and put out of action. Two German A7V tanks were recognized, No.525 'Siegfried' and later No.504 'Schnuck'. 'Siegfried' was first on the scene, commanded by 2nd Leutnant Bitter, but his gun was giving trouble. 'Schnuck', commanded by 2nd Leutnant Muller, came up later, but the Whippets were also under fire from 2nd Battery, 6th Guards Field Regiment, whose 77mm guns were more than capable of destroying a Whippet if they achieved a hit. It is not clear where the fire came from that knocked out the Whippets. A number of men from X Company were wounded in the actions, but only the crew of one tank, A256, were reported as missing. They were 2nd Lieutenant H. Dale and his crew Lance Corporal Lincoln and Gunner Herbert. Dale appears to have been killed, although the other two men were

C

1: WHIPPET A277 OF X COMPANY, 3rd BATTALION TANK CORPS AT VILLERS-BRETONNEUX, 24 APRIL 1918

This illustration is taken from a painting of the tank commanded by Sergeant C. Parrott during the action near Cachy. The improvised X Company was commanded by Temporary Captain Tommy Price, and consisted of seven Whippet tanks. At 10.30am it was lying up in a wood, the Bois de Blangy, when Price was told by 58th Division that a message, dropped by an aircraft, reported two battalions of German infantry forming up for an attack. Price was ordered to go in and break up the attack. Price himself was on a horse so he left the tanks in a hollow, with their engines running, while he went forward to investigate. Having seen that the open country was ideal for tanks he galloped back and ordered them to charge, due south, at full speed.

The tanks drove through the Germans with machine guns blazing and running over many troops, then turned and did the same thing again. Regarding the painting, Price took care to point out that the letter P on the tank stood for Parrott, not Price. Note the excellent view of the six central weight-bearing track rollers with their Skefco roller-bearing covers that distinguish a production Medium A from the prototype.

2: MEDIUM A WHIPPET *THE MUSICAL BOX* OF B COMPANY, 6th BATTALION, TANK CORPS

Near Amiens on 8 August 1918 this tank, commanded by Lieutenant C. B. Arnold with his crew comprising Driver W. J. Carnie and Gunner C. Ribbans, became separated from 9th Cavalry Brigade. Very soon he was well ahead of the advancing British troops and overtaking the tail of the retreating Germans. He cut down many with his machine guns but also came under intense rifle and machine-gun fire in return. The tank had been carrying extra cans of petrol on the roof, and when these were holed the petrol ran down inside the crew compartment and made breathing difficult. Eventually the tank caught fire and as they evacuated Driver Carnie was shot and killed. Lieutenant Arnold and Gunner Ribbans finished the war as prisoners of war in Germany. Their partially burnt-out tank was found abandoned the next day with no clue as to what had happened to the crew.

1

2

Chinese workers hosing and cleaning down a Whippet at the Tank Corps Depot. It would have come in from the field liberally covered in mud. Whether the tank's number has been blotted out by the censor for security reasons is not clear, but it seems to be a pointless act.

probably taken prisoner. In all, X Company seems to have suffered six men wounded and one killed for the loss of four tanks out of a total of 21 men and seven tanks engaged, which is not too bad when weighed against the decimation of two battalions. Even if the number of enemy killed was not as many as 400, there is no doubt that after the action neither battalion was fit to fight again.

The following day, 25 April, Price was ordered to send his three remaining tanks to ascertain the situation. He discovered a shallow trench crowded with German infantry just west of a road in the area. His three tanks cruised along the road, firing into the trench with their machine guns and doing some execution. However, they also came under fire from a mass of enemy machine guns, and, although these machine guns were not firing armour piercing rounds, they did manage to wound two crew members, Sergeant Hibbert and Gunner Stone, although both remained at their duty. All three tanks survived, although Price concluded his report by saying 'I consider that a low flying aeroplane would have been able to carry out this reconnaissance more effectively'.

The following day Tommy Price himself was wounded. He had gone with 2nd Lieutenant Ritchie to examine one of the abandoned tanks on the Cachy battlefield when a machine gun opened up from inside the tank, wounding both officers as they approached. The infantry had informed them that the nearest Germans were 2,000 yards away. What was left of X Company was relieved by C Company, 9th Battalion on 28 April.

May 1918 seems to have been a relatively quiet month for the 3rd Battalion, although they were often held in readiness if a German attack began. All three companies had now come together again, and could muster 43 Whippet tanks between them. On 3 May they received a visit from Major Giffard le Q. Martel from Tank Corps headquarters, who came to observe the installation

A Whippet on the driving area, along with Mark V tanks at the Tank Corps Depot in France. It may be there for testing after being repaired, or just for crew familiarization. Most of the other tanks on the area are of the Mark V type. The bare trees suggest a winter scene, while the red and white stripes indicate late spring at the earliest.

of explosive devices in tanks that were to be used for the purposes of demolition if the tank had to be abandoned or was in danger of being captured. Then on 25 May it was announced that in future C Company, 9th Battalion, attached to the 3rd Battalion, would be known as D Company, 3rd Battalion, but not for long.

The commanding officer of 3rd Battalion, Lieutenant Colonel S. H. Charrington, made the point firmly in one of his instructions that the tactical unit for light tanks was the Company, and that tanks should not be employed in smaller numbers than this. In a later report, he pointed out that as the British extended their trench system, and because

Whippet tanks being prepared for action near Albert on 28 March 1918. Notice how detachable track spuds have been slung across the back; this was not the usual place to find them, but was a lot safer in an emergency than clipped to the side. Other evidence suggests that they did not make much difference to the tank's performance.

in many places the trenches were impassable to light tanks, reconnaissance of routes became of the utmost importance. Towards the end of May, 3rd Battalion was involved in a major exercise with the 113th and 115th brigades. It is instructive to note that this involved co-operation with infantry alone and that cavalry was not mentioned at all.

On 31 May, three Whippets from 3rd Battalion were involved in trench crossing trials near Puchvillers, the results of which were very instructive. Two trenches were selected. Trench A was 10ft wide at the top by up to 8ft deep, and Trench B was 10ft 3in wide at the top and 7ft 6in deep. They immediately discovered that the depth of the trench made no difference at all, but the width did. On Trench A the three tanks crossed easily in both directions, while Trench B proved impassable. Here, as a tank proceeded across and lost its grip on the near side, the back of the tank slid backwards into the trench until it came to rest, nearly vertical. The only way to get it out was to hitch another tank onto the front by rope and haul it until it was nearly level, at which point the engines could be restarted and the tank

A Whippet that appears to be from Lieutenant Sewell's section, apparently working with the French. It also has a cluster of fuel cans roped onto the front and a small mountain of other stowage in the boxes on the back and on the cab roof. No weapons are mounted but the black stripes painted on the cab are there to disguise the location of vision slits.

The Medium A was a complex and difficult tank for one man to drive. Each of the controls had to be duplicated to suit each engine, all the way back to the tracks. It was not helped by the fact that one had to double-declutch on two gearboxes, going both up and down the box. It was said that if one had been a professional juggler on the stage before the war one had the correct coordination; otherwise one had to learn the hard way. To make matters worse, conditions in the small cab were appalling, with the heat and fumes blowing back off the engines, so that each tank needed two crews to work on alternate days. Even so in skilled hands the tank was quite fast and very manoeuvrable, although that did not prevent quite a few of them from being knocked out by artillery fire during the war.

KEY

1. Hinged engine cover
2. Radiators
3. Fan casing, starboard side
4. Radiator cooling fan, starboard side
5. Forward, offside, track guard support strut
6. Armour protected petrol tank
7. Track tension adjuster
8. White/Red/White Allied recognition mark
9. Engine compartment ventilation louvre
10. Offside exhaust pipe and silencer
11. Hot water pipe to radiator
12. Tylor 45hp, four cylinder engine, starboard side
13. Engine flywheel and clutch, starboard side
14. Plain track roller spindle
15. Skefco roller bearing cover
16. Spare track spud
17. Track side mud chute
18. Track return roller
19. Clutch pedal, starboard side
20. Gear shift lever for starboard gearbox
21. Driver's seat
22. Starboard gearbox
23. Final drive sprocket bearing cap, starboard side
24. Final drive chain, starboard side
25. Track drive sprocket, starboard side
26. Drive sprocket bearing cap
27. Track link, 6mm armour
28. Worm drive casing, starboard side
29. Detachable track spuds
30. Nearside rear track guard support strut
31. Gearbox output shaft, port side
32. Rack for boxes of Hotchkiss ammunition
33. Rear mounted Hotchkiss .303-inch air-cooled machine gun
34. Machine-gunner's vision slit
35. Rear access door
36. Hotchkiss .303-inch machine gun in ball mount, port side
37. Loophole or pistol port with armoured cover
38. Commander's roof hatch
39. Forward mounted Hotchkiss machine-gun
40. Autovac petrol supply system
41. Brake levers
42. Gear shift, port side
43. Throttle control hand wheel

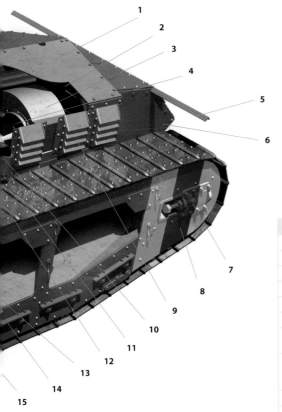

Technical Data (from official figures)	
Crew	three
Weight	14 tons
Power to weight ratio	6.43:1
Overall length	20ft
Overall width	8ft 7in
Overall height	9ft
Engines	Two Tylor four-cylinder 45hp water cooled, petrol, revving at 1,250rpm
Transmission	Cone clutch to four-speed and reverse gearbox to worm reduction and bevel drive, chain loop to drive sprocket, one for each track
Fuel capacity	70 gallons
Max speed	8.3mph
Radius of action	80 miles
Ground pressure	15.8 lb per square inch
Trench crossing capability	8ft 6in
Armament	Four Hotchkiss .303-inch, air-cooled machine guns
Ammunition stowage	5,400 rounds

Two Whippets named *Comme Ci* and *Comme Ca* served with 3rd Battalion during the war. *Comme Ca* is shown here; the name of the other tank cannot be confirmed. Both tanks look semi-derelict and abandoned, although what appears to be an engine starting handle can be seen at the back of the tank on the left.

driven out with a bit of help from the towing tank. Attempts to make the crossing easier by digging ramps on the lips of the trenches made no difference. Captain May noted that when spuds were fitted to the tracks they barely had any effect at all. Who could have believed that a mere 3in would make so much difference?

In June, the battalion was increased by the addition of four Mark IV supply or baggage tanks, which were handed over to B Company on the 14th. On 20 June, it was announced that D Company, all of 26 days old, would no longer be known as such, but was to become the nucleus of the Battalion Driving School that was being established at the Bois Monsieur, near Talmas. Meanwhile it appears that 9th Battalion had already established a new C Company, equipped with Mark V tanks. It seems, at least from June onwards, that the old C Company, the Whippet Company, simply ceased to exist.

Nothing much else happened in June except that the entire battalion was stricken by influenza, but in July a series of experiments were carried out involving co-operation with the Royal Air Force (RAF). This involved 8 Squadron RAF (commanded by Trafford Leigh-Mallory), notably A Flight. Despite Tank Corps officers going up in aircraft and RAF officers travelling in tanks, it soon became clear that spotting an aircraft from a tank was difficult enough, never mind using it to obtain directions. However, 8 Squadron was established as a dedicated tank liaison squadron, so experiments continued.

Meanwhile, another battalion had appeared on the Whippet scene. 6th Battalion had started to receive a few Whippets in December 1917, and more in January 1918, but training had never really got under way becaue of the German spring offensive, preceded by complications due to inclement weather and a shortage of men, as replacements were still needed after the losses of the Cambrai battle. Except for the part the battalion played in countering the German offensive, which was largely a passive one, no more Whippet activity occurred until 15 June, when it finally handed in its old Mark IV tanks and six days later arrived by bus at Merlimont to commence Whippet training.

Photographed near Paddock Wood on the South-Eastern and Chatham Railway, a trainload of Whippets returning from the war. Four of them appear to have their back doors open. The train is said to be destined for Aldershot, but this may be no more than a guess. Bovington would seem more likely.

Conditions at Merlimont, on the Channel coast, were not good, with a lot of fine sand blowing about, while high midsummer temperatures meant that conditions inside the cab of a Whippet were worse than ever. Dealing with the sand demanded a lot of ingenuity, but nothing could be done about the heat. Training was carried out on driving and on the Hotchkiss machine gun. Since the crew of a Whippet amounted to only two other ranks, in addition to the officer or NCO in command, it was regarded as essential that the men were all trained to drive and fight, although at the end of their training it was decided which men made the most promising drivers or machine-gunners and they were given their roles accordingly. Trials at Merlimont were also carried out in tank/air cooperation, but the results were no better than for 3rd Battalion.

The battle of Amiens (8 August 1918) saw both Whippet battalions in action. The action began for both battalions with their moving into Amiens itself for an overnight stay on the eve of the battle. 3rd Battalion was directed to the Boulevard Pont Noyelles, where it parked up under the trees and the men were installed in adjacent billets for the night. 6th Battalion was directed to a boulevard that led out of the city in the direction of Villers Bretonneux, and the men were billeted in a nearby school. There were strict warnings in place concerning the risks of enemy aerial reconnaissance. Nobody was tomove or congregate near the tanks, no fires were to be lit outdoors, and men were to stay in their billets until it was time to go.

3rd Battalion started to move away from Amiens just before 9pm, followed by 6th Battalion, which started off about midnight. 3rd Battalion was to meet up with the 3rd Cavalry Brigade, which it was supposed to be supporting, while 6th Battalion was supporting the 9th Cavalry Brigade, but it is instructive to note that no combined training had been arranged beforehand and the extent to which either battalion could effectively assist the cavalry was worked out with senior cavalry officers only shortly before they moved off. One gets the impression that nobody had any great faith in the efficacy of this arrangement.

Rather than follow the experiences of these two battalions over the period of the Amiens battle, perhaps it would be more instructive to examine their general experiences with the cavalry, since, except on rare occasions, it was not repeated. The idea was that the first stage of the battle would be conducted by infantry divisions, supported by Mark V tanks, whose objective, known as the Red Line, was the second objective, about two miles from the start line. At this point the cavalry would take over, assisted by the Whippets, and race on to take the third objective, the Outer Amiens Defence Line.

6th Battalion summed up its experiences on the day by saying, in a marginal note in its history, 'Whippets not suitable for co-operation with Cavalry'. It went on to point out that either the cavalry wanted to advance at the gallop, leaving the Whippets behind, or the Whippets would move forward in the face of machine-gun fire, while the cavalry had to dismount and seek cover. The battalion also pointed out that when the Whippets came to take over the advance, they were obliged to operate over a great frontage and depth, so that even companies became scattered. Before long they were broken down into individual sections and the section became the unit, which was in direct opposition to Colonel Charrington's earlier directive. Because they were so scattered, and the distances were great, the only way senior officers such as company commanders could keep in touch was if they were mounted on horses, which accounted for the high casualty rate amongst them. Conversely, section commanders had to travel in one of their tanks in order to keep up, which made it difficult for them to maintain control.

Cavalry also had an unfortunate habit of wandering off along routes such as sunken lanes, which often took them away from the direction of attack. It also seems that they were not aware of the limitations of the tanks. For instance, a composite section of seven tanks under Captain J. A. Renwick, after losing one tank to artillery fire, was directed over a segment of the old Somme trench system, where most of the trenches were overgrown and in a dilapidated state. All of the surviving six tanks became bogged and three were subsequently knocked out by artillery fire. Meanwhile the other composite section, under Captain Chapman, found itself being directed along the Parvillers road, which, from a reconnaissance on foot, they found to be covered by two German field guns that would have been able to fire at point-blank range at any approaching tanks. There were also a number of occasions when tanks were sent to meet up with a cavalry detachment at a particular point only to find themselves alone.

Following one more successful action with the Queens Bays, two tanks finally broke away and went hunting on their own. One of these tanks, commanded by Lieutenant C. B. Arnold, became involved in clearing up an artillery battery in front of the 60th Australian Brigade, and then, having become separated from the other tank, went on a wild spree, shooting up enemy transport and troops at various locations before finally being knocked out and captured.

In the aftermath of the first three days of Amiens, the Whippet tanks seem to have been used for more general work, mostly in support of infantry. In the main, they used their mobility to attack nests of machine guns that were holding up the infantry. As they did so, there was a notable increase in tank casualties. Tanks were struck by artillery and destroyed by fire, which often included the crew. Although they continued to use crews on alternating days, this still meant that the tanks were being employed on a daily basis, with precious little time to spare for maintenance. As a result, there were increasing instances of tanks breaking down, owing to simple things such as the fan drive breaking to more fundamental failures such as the complete collapse of engine components, particularly the big end. Heat continued to be a problem, and not only for the crew. Colonel Charrington, writing in the 3rd Battalion War Diary on 24 August 1918, pointed out that one hour's running with the door shut could render a tank weaponless except for the crew's revolvers. In the hot interior, machine guns would jam as rounds expanded or even exploded, and often the gun itself became too hot to handle. On one occasion the steering wheel became too hot to touch.

3rd Battalion latterly worked in conjunction with New Zealand, Australian and American forces, but supporting them in the infantry role, not as cavalry. Although it was noted that on certain occasions a heavy tank, like a Mark V, would have been more suitable, Whippet commanders found that,

A Whippet captured and put into working order by the Germans. It never saw operational use during the war, but was regarded as the best model for the Germans to copy. As far as is known, the Germans only ever acquired two Whippet tanks, at least in running condition.

if used cleverly and taking advantage of their manoeuvrability, they could outflank and destroy enemy machine-gun or artillery batteries. When used individually, the tanks were more vulnerable, and many were destroyed by direct hits, with the crew often lost as well.

There was a dramatic incident on 29 August, when Lieutenant Cecil Sewell rescued the crew of another tank in his section at the cost of his life, resulting in the posthumous award of the Victoria Cross. Actions continued, with every available spare moment given over to tank maintenance and with a dwindling number of serviceable tanks available. On 20 September, the entire 3rd Battalion could muster only 31 Whippets fit for action, and, of these, the tanks of B Company were allocated to work in conjunction with the Austin armoured cars of 17th (Armoured Car) Battalion, Tank Corps in an attack on the village of Bony. This failed, partly because on reaching the agreed meeting point the tanks found that the armoured cars had gone on ahead, but also because the intensity of enemy fire that they encountered, when they finally followed in the wake of the armoured cars, was so great that they had to withdraw, and in subsequent discussions it was agreed to call this interesting experiment off. The battalion's last attack in the war was against Serain on 8 October, when the commanding officer reported that in his view it was a task more suited to heavy tanks. The battalion was down to 11 tanks on this occasion. By the end of that month, the battalion was using Mark V tanks for training, and on 28 October it finally handed all its Whippets in to central workshops and started upon the new training programme.

Not an easy shot, but the only one showing the Whippet prototype with a set of tail wheels. This prototype was seen at Dollis Hill and photographed across the tail of a gun carrier machine. Many of the staff at Dollis Hill appear to be Royal Naval personnel, perhaps members of 20 Squadron R.N.A.S.

There is an interesting account, told differently in the *Sixth Battalion History* and the *Tank Corps Book of Honour*, concerning Private Bertie Bussey, a Whippet driver who, on 23 August 1918, after the officer and sergeant in his tank had both been wounded, alternately drove his tank and worked the machine guns – with the transmission locked – in action for about four hours until he was discovered and sent back to the rallying point. Private Bussey received the Distinguished Conduct Medal for his efforts.

6th Battalion had acquired its own Victoria Cross hero, also posthumously, in the shape of their commanding officer, acting Lieutenant-Colonel R. A. West, who had already earned a DSO (Distinguished Service Order) and MC (Military Cross). West, while riding forward to ascertain the best time to use his Whippets on 2 September 1918, came across the remains of an infantry battalion with most of its officers already dead and about to receive a strong counter-attack. West managed to inspire the men by riding his horse in front of them, but was killed in the process, although the attack was defeated. However, this had nothing to do with Whippet tanks. The following day, six

The Medium A Whippet modified by Philip Johnson for high speed running, with sprung suspension, a 360hp Rolls-Royce Eagle engine, and Mark V transmission. In this form it is reputed to have achieved 30mph. Quite where it was photographed is uncertain.

Whippets were attached to A Squadron, Queen's Own Oxfordshire Hussars. This was the last occasion when they would work with cavalry, and it is interesting that when the advancing tanks passed through the villages of Hermies and Dermicourt, they found them free of Germans, yet, when the cavalry advanced, they encountered machine-gun fire coming from Dermicourt and lost three horses. This suggests that the enemy laid low when the tanks were nearby, but came to life again when a more

A Whippet tank handed over to Commander Bayntum Hippisely RN for undisclosed experiments, photographed outside his house at Ston Easton near Bath. There is no obvious evidence of modification on the outside, so one assumes that whatever the commander was doing concerned the inside.

suitable target approached.

For the final few weeks of the war, 6th Battalion, like the 3rd, was gradually reduced to the point where composite companies had to be formed for specific operations. However, for various reasons, but largely due to luck, the 3rd Battalion does not appear to have suffered so many casualties. Its final action of the war began on 5 November in conjunction with the Scots and Grenadier Guards. It was only partially successful, but resulted in the Germans retreating overnight, and for the next few days what remained of the battalion was engaged in moving to a new location and working on its surviving tanks until the Armistice was announced on 11 November.

Julian's Baby

A217 *Julian's Baby* is the only Whippet tank known to have participated in the National War Savings Committee campaign for the sale of war bonds. Commanded by Lieutenant E. A. Collett of the 22nd Light Tank Battalion, its name clearly derives from the Mark IV touring tank *Julian*, which was already well known in the north of England, Scotland and the Borders.

Julian's Baby toured from Glasgow to Edinburgh via Duns in the early months of 1919, which must have been a gruelling experience for the crew. Even with the rear door open, heat and fumes wafting back from the engine compartment could be very debilitating.

The 22nd Light Tank Battalion would have been destined to operate medium tanks had the war continued into 1919, albeit with Medium C Hornet tanks rather than the Medium A Whippet that Collett commanded. Indeed, a detachment from the battalion took a couple of Medium C tanks to Liverpool at the time of the police strike.

Collett's trip was deemed to be a success, since he received a complimentary letter from the Scottish War Savings Committee from its offices in Edinburgh dated 14 March 1919.

WHIPPETS ABROAD

With the ending of the war, some Whippet tanks emigrated. Some went to trouble spots where problems had arisen as a result of the war. Others were purchased by countries anxious to avail themselves of the new technology, while a few more were acquired by allies who thought they would make interesting memorials, particularly if their armies had seen action alongside British tanks and wanted a tangible reminder of the connection. At least two had been acquired by the Germans, which they proposed to use until they were repossessed.

The Japanese obtained three or four Whippets, along with a Mark IV and some French Renaults, which they intended to evaluate and train with. They do not appear to have lasted very long. The Japanese Army fitted its own machine guns that were derived from the French Hotchkiss, and adapted the armoured panel in front of the driver so that it hinged upwards. This not only gave him a better view ahead, as far as that was possible, but it also helped to ventilate the fighting compartment, which was badly needed. The British Army took 16 Whippets to Ireland, where initially they formed B Company, 17th (Armoured Car) Battalion Tank Corps, which had been rushed across to Ireland from Germany at the end of the war. In due course they seem to have been sent far and wide throughout the country along with an interesting mixture of other tanks and armoured cars. For instance, two Whippets along with a Mark IV male tank and two Austin armoured cars formed Number 2 Detachment, Tank Corps based at Cork in 1919, while four took part in the victory parade through Dublin that summer. Six went with the British military mission of April 1919 to Russia in support of General Denikin, whose White Russians, bolstered by Allied help, were attempting to counter the Bolsheviks and their Red Revolution. Once it became obvious that this was going to be a more daunting task, a much larger detachment of tanks including more Whippets arrived in July 1919 and formed the South Russian Tank Detachment, which had the duty of training White Russian tank crews. This seems to have been a thankless task, because morale was low and the Revolutionary movement too strong. The men of the South Russian Tank Detachment were subsequently pulled out of the country, the tanks having been handed over to their White Russian crews. These did not last very long either, and the tanks were then captured and formed a substantial part of the rapidly expanding Red Army. They saw some action against the Poles in the West, the Japanese in the East, and dissident groups within Russia itself. There is some evidence that at least one Whippet had been modified to mount a 37mm gun from a Renault, much as had been done by the British, and it is said that in Red Army service they were known as Teiylors, on account of their Tylor engines. However, it seems that the survivors only lasted until about 1922.

The Union of South Africa purchased one Whippet, which was named H. M. L. S. *Union*. It was intended as a memorial, although it seems to have been wheeled out during an industrial dispute in the hope that it might overawe the agitators. Unfortunately it broke down

Whippets leading the Victory Parade in Dublin in 1919, followed by three Mark V* tanks. The Whippets were named *Fanny Adams*, *Fanny's Sister*, *Golikell* and *Gofasta* (i.e 'Go Like Hell' and 'Go Faster').

and had to be towed home somewhat ignominiously behind a steam lorry. Individual Whippet tanks were also sent to Canada and the United States.

In addition to the immovable wrecks captured by the Germans at Bray-sur-Somme, which had been too drastically damaged to be worth restoring, two more evidently fell into German hands in somewhat better order. Both were put back into working order by the Bayerischer Armee-Kraftwagen-Park 20 (BAKP20), which had established a tank repair facility in captured factory premises near Charleroi in occupied Belgium. One was delivered to Berlin, while BAKP20 retained the other for evaluation. A German officer commanding the captured tank force is reported to have said that in his opinion the Whippet was the only British tank worth copying, which may explain the design of the German tanks LKI and LKII. Both were completed too late to be of any material use during the war, and in any case suffered from the German commitment to engineering perfection, which delayed their completion until it was too late. The other Whippet, the one that went to Berlin, was photographed in Freikorps service during the street fighting against the Communist-inspired Spartacist movement in January 1919. Both tanks had to be handed over to British troops in the summer of 1919 when Germany finally surrendered.

MEDIUM B

Nobody would argue that the Medium A Whippet needed replacing. The location of the crew compartment, the truly appalling conditions inflicted on the men, the complicated driving arrangements, poor driver visibility, and the extra time required to keep both engines in trim (thus doubling up

1: MEDIUM A WHIPPET *CAESAR II*

Lieutenant Cecil Sewell began his military career with the Royal West Kent Regiment and ended it a short time later with the 3rd (Light) Battalion, Tank Corps. Sewell was killed on 29 August 1918, earning a posthumous Victoria Cross in the process. Sewell had been a tank commander at Cambrai in November 1917, and when he was killed he was a section commander in overall charge of four Whippet tanks, including his own Whippet A259, *Caesar II*. On the afternoon of 29 August his section was sent forward to deal with German troops near Frémicourt. As they advanced under intense rifle and machine-gun fire one of Sewell's tanks, Whippet A233 under the command of Lieutenant O. L. Rees-Williams, slipped off the road and turned upside down in a shell crater, falling in such a way that the rear door, the only means of escape, was jammed shut by mud. To make matters worse the disabled tank caught fire, threatening to burn the three-man crew alive.

Sewell jumped down from his tank and, grabbing a shovel, ran across to the inverted tank in a hail of bullets. He dug the mud away from the door, enabling the three men, who had already put the fire out, to escape. Meanwhile Sewell's driver, W. Knox, had jumped out intending to help, but was wounded immediately. Sewell ran back to him but was killed in the process, as was Driver Knox. Their tank *Caesar II* is now an exhibit in the Tank Museum, having been there since 1949.

2: MEDIUM A WHIPPET *LOVE CHILD*, SOUTH RUSSIAN TANK DETACHMENT, 1919

The South Russian Tank Detachment was formed in France after the Armistice. It arrived in Batum on the Black Sea coast on 13 April 1919 where it was joined by a second detachment equipped with six Mark V heavy tanks and six Medium A Whippets, all under the command of Major Neil McMicking DSO. They were there to support the White Russians under General Denikin, in the civil war against the Bolsheviks. They were later reinforced by about 50 more Mark V tanks and ten Whippets, which were handed over to the Russians.

This tank, nicknamed 'Love Child' was photographed manned by a British crew. When White Russian resistance collapsed and the British left, in June 1920 the tanks were taken over by the Bolsheviks; in Red Army service the Whippets were apparently known as Tyeilors after their Tylor 45hp engines.

1

CAESAR II

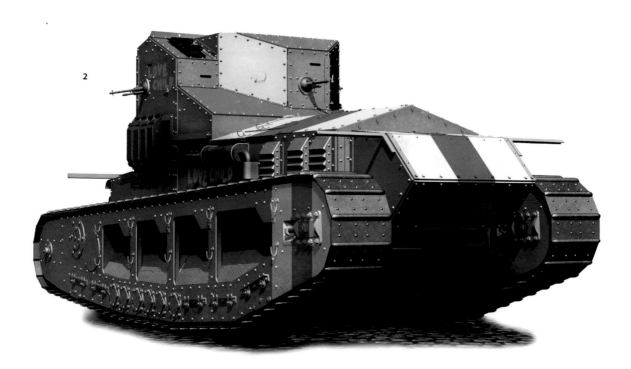

2

An early example of a Medium B built by the Coventry Ordnance Works, still to be fitted with the driver's cab. Notice the machine-gun mountings in the superstructure and in the side door. These tanks could also mount an anti-aircraft machine gun if required.

maintenance time) were more than enough to condemn it in the eyes of those who had to use it.

Walter Wilson's tank design, created in June 1917, was bound to feature his transmission but, in an effort to reduce the size, he elected to use a shorter, four-cylinder version of the Ricardo engine rated at 100hp, many of which were manufactured by Browett, Lindley & Co of Patricroft, Manchester. Wilson opted for a hull design reminiscent of a heavy tank with a rounded nose and much higher entry point, which gave improved cross-country performance. He moved the crew compartment forward so that the driver was placed centrally, right at the front with the fighting compartment above and behind him. This included five ball mountings for Hotchkiss machine guns: two facing forwards, one to the rear, and one each side, along with the usual selection of pistol ports and vision slits. A double flap hatch was fitted in the cab roof for the commander to observe through, but no cupola was provided, although a trunnion could be fitted to support an anti-aircraft machine gun. Access doors stuck out on each side, looking like small sponsons. Each one of these was also provided with a ball mounting for a Hotchkiss machine gun,

A Medium B from the batch built by the Metropolitan Carriage, Wagon and Finance Company. Note that the machine-gun mounting on the side door has been blanked off. This rear view shows the long sloping engine deck, the location of the silencer, and the exhaust pipe.

although this was subsequently removed. The tall central superstructure meant that it would be impossible to use a conventional unditching beam with this tank, so since some form of unditching apparatus was considered essential, the designers reverted to an earlier type, the Buddicom unditching spud, of which a pair was used, attached to the track on either side and flexible enough to slide by the superstructure as they went around. Since this system never seemed to work properly on earlier tanks, it is not clear how well it might have behaved on these later medium tanks, but since no photographs have yet been found showing them being used on a Medium B, this remains a bit of a puzzle.

A Medium B photographed with a Tank Corps soldier, although where and under what circumstances is unknown. However, this tank still has the machine-gun mountings in the side doors, so it must be an early example. The hatch in the cab roof is also open.

The engine was placed on the centre line of the hull directly in the rear of the fighting compartment, since it was important that it was set as far back as possible. Being a typical Ricardo design it was quite tall, which necessitated a slightly raised engine deck above the level of the top run of the tracks. It was water cooled with the radiator located in the left side, and petrol delivered to the engine by the Autovac system was carried in three petrol tanks low down at the very rear of the hull. The exhaust from the engine was led into a silencer mounted crosswise, and an outlet pipe carried the fumes down to the back of the tank. A device was fitted that injected sulphonic acid into the exhaust to create a smoke screen. Total fuel capacity was 85 gallons and fuel was consumed at a rate of ¾ miles per gallon, which gave the Medium B a range of about 64 miles.

Behind the engine was the typical combination of a four-speed and reverse gearbox, which was described as unreliable in practice, and a bevel box with pinions and gears linked to Wilson epicyclics at their outboard ends for steering. Chains then carried the motion back to the final drive sprockets, which meshed with the tracks. In top gear, the tank could manage just over 6mph. This was slower by 2mph than the Medium A, but the Medium B was 4 tons heavier at 18 tons and of course a lot easier to drive, particularly in Terms of steering, which must have made a lot of difference.

Conditions for the crew inside were a lot better, since the engine was separated from the fighting compartment by a bulkhead with doors giving access to each side, but Wilson was severely criticized for the cramped conditions within the engine compartment, which meant that anyone trying to work in there with the engine running or just stopped ran the risk of being roasted alive. This could make a crucial difference if a tank were to break down on the battlefield.

Orders were placed for some 700 machines with the Metropolitan Carriage, Wagon and Finance Company in Birmingham through their subsidiary the Patent Shaft and Axletree Company of Wednesbury (although this order was soon cancelled) and with the North British Locomotive Company and the Coventry Ordnance Works in Glasgow. The prototype, which was completed by September 1918, was built in Birmingham, presumably where Wilson could keep an eye on it. However, the first production tank appeared from the Coventry Ordnance Works.

One Medium B, originally part of the British North Russian Tank Detachment, ended up in Latvia and is seen on parade in Riga with some Mark V tanks from the same source. Ultimately it must have fallen into Soviet hands, and here is still apparently in excellent condition.

All told, some 102 Medium B tanks were completed, and the number sequences seen in photographs suggest that some of them were built by all three contractors. Of these, 45 were taken into service and the remainder scrapped. It is not clear how many were completed by each contractor.

A version of the Medium B was proposed to mount a 2-pdr gun. However, this must have been an entirely new weapon and not the automatic Vickers Pom-Pom. References claim that design work on the 2-pdr held up production of the 6-pdr gun fitted in male heavy tanks, but where this new weapon might have been mounted in a male Medium B is not recorded. In any case the project was abandoned in March 1918.

The post-war career of this all but forgotten tank is not well recorded. An unspecified number were shipped to Dublin to join C Company, 17th Battalion Tank Corps, which was based there, but little is known about them and no

F

1: MEDIUM B

This tank had an interesting career. On entering Tank Corps service it was issued to the North Russian Tank Detachment, which sailed for Archangel in August 1919. It was then passed on to the Latvian Army but subsequently fell into Bolshevik hands and entered service with the Red Army, finished in the rather colourful camouflage pattern depicted here.

Medium B tanks were built by Metropolitan in Birmingham, the Coventry Ordnance Works and North British Locomotive Company in Glasgow. Out of 700 ordered only 45 ever entered service, and none survive now. This tank cannot have lasted long in Soviet use, being a difficult tank for the crew to operate. It is shown fully equipped with air-cooled Hotchkiss machine guns.

2: MEDIUM C 'THE HORNET'

The Medium C was always reckoned to be the best British tank of World War I although it had never been in action nor served overseas at all. It was, however, the culmination of all that was best in tank design by World War I standards. Out of 50 built, 36 were taken into Tank Corps service after the war. However, at one point when it looked as if the war would continue into 1919, 600 Medium Cs were on order, all from William Foster & Co, of Lincoln. Of the tanks built, 24 were issued to 2nd Battalion, Tank Corps, then based at Farnborough, but were all replaced by more modern tanks by about 1923.

Designed by Sir William Tritton and nicknamed 'the Hornet', the prototype was completed in August 1918, but production tanks were not expected to be ready for delivery before January 1919. They were big tanks, similar in size to a heavy tank, but only required a crew of four, two of whom had to manage up to five machine guns between them. However, at 20 tons they were a good deal lighter than a heavy tank (which weighed around 28 tons) and they had a respectable top speed of nearly 8mph. The highlight of their military career seems to have been in July 1919 when four Medium C tanks were selected to represent the Tank Corps in the London Victory Parade.

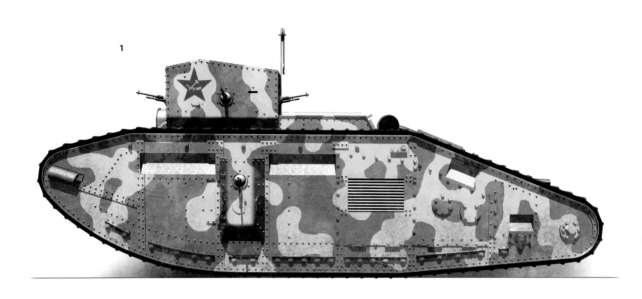

1

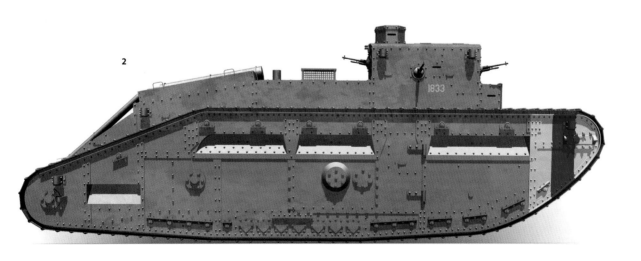

2

photographs have come to light, suggesting that there were not many of them and they were rarely used. Three Medium Bs were shipped out to Archangel to join the North British Tank Detachment, which was stationed there to protect the port and vast stocks of British supplies from falling into the hands of the Bolsheviks. Of these three, one tank and a Mark V heavy model were passed on to White Russian forces, who reputedly used them quite effectively. However, when the Bolsheviks closed in they refused to surrender them and reportedly sunk the tanks in the Dvina River; the other two were handed over to the Latvian Army when the British pulled out in October 1919, and one of these was still in Latvian service in 1926. However, photographic evidence suggests that one Medium B fell into Bolshevik hands and was put back into working order in Moscow; its ultimate fate is not known.

In Britain, at least one Medium B was issued to the Royal Engineers Experimental Bridging Establishment at Christchurch, where it was used to test new bridges. This tank, or a similar one, was seen on 23 January 1941 at Christchurch, stripped of most of its internal fittings as part of the test load for a Mark III Inglis bridge, but this was wartime and it did not survive. A few Medium B tanks must have remained at locations such as Bovington, but none ever seem to have entered battalion service apart from those in Ireland. In due course they were presumably all scrapped except for one, earmarked for the original Tank Museum collection, which ultimately also went for scrap. Perhaps this is a comment on its perceived significance.

MEDIUM C: THE HORNET

If one ignores Foster's propaganda and accepts official information, then design of the Medium C commenced in March 1918, about nine months after the Medium B and only a month after the first production example of Wilson's tank had been delivered. This raises a number of questions. Assuming this was before faults with the Medium B became obvious, why did the designers bother with a new model? And why in any case did not Tritton and Wilson co-operate on the design following the success of their earlier partnership? There is no evidence to suggest that they had fallen out. On the other hand, it was clear that Tritton's earlier design, the Medium A, was not entirely satisfactory, and Wilson as the inventor of the epicyclic

This is the only known photograph of a Medium B and Medium C tank together. It was taken at Bovington during a parade for the General Officer Commanding Southern Command in May 1919. The rail on the side of the Medium B was intended to prevent the machine gun from firing into the hull.

Photographed on the waste ground adjacent to Foster's factory in Lincoln, this is the Medium C Hornet prototype being put through its paces. Notice in particular the commander's cupola on top of the superstructure. This gave the tank commander an all-round view of the battlefield.

steering system probably thought that he could do better. Maybe the authorities felt they should have two strings to their bow, namely the inventive genius of Wilson and Tritton the experienced engineer with excellent manufacturing facilities at his back.

We will probably never know for sure. Both tanks were similar in design, although the Medium C was the larger; indeed, it was longer and taller by a few inches than the old heavy tank of 1916, but not as wide since it did not carry sponsons. One feature that Tritton made much of was the fact that the crew compartment was a much healthier place; in fact, it was not much warmer than the ambient temperature outside. This may also have been true of the Medium B, but since Tritton made more of it, the suggestion is that he was well aware of the problems with the Medium A and wanted to advertise the fact that he had overcome them.

The crew of the Medium C came to four: a commander, driver, and two gunners, as in the Medium B. However, the gunners would have been kept busy in action. There were two Hotchkiss machine-gun mountings in the front of the superstructure, above the driver's head, one in each side of the superstructure and one more at the back, along with one that could be fitted to a trunnion mounting in the roof hatch for anti-aircraft use when required. There was also a pistol port at the very back of the tank, alongside a small escape door. The gunner would have had to make his way down a narrow corridor at the side of the engine to reach it and was then cut off entirely from the rest of the crew.

A Medium C belonging to 2nd Battalion, Tank Corps, seen going over the level crossing at Farnham in Surrey. This seems to have been quite a favourite route for the tanks, which were based at Aldershot. 2nd Battalion retained the Medium C right up to the time that it was issued with the new medium tanks early in 1924.

This Medium C tank was displayed in the original open-air Tank Museum at Bovington Camp. Sitting alongside it is the Medium D* prototype. If the figure on the print is the date the photo was taken, then they are two of the tanks not scheduled to be included in the new museum, and were unfortunately scrapped.

The commander on the other hand was provided with a rotating cupola, or lookout turret as it was called then, high up on the roof of the superstructure that gave him an uninterrupted view all around the tank. The only drawback was that this had to be removed for rail travel, since it exceeded the railway loading gauge. Once again the central superstructure of the Medium C meant that a conventional unditching beam could not be used, and reports suggest that individual torpedo spuds were provided instead; however, the same problem would have applied as indicated for the Medium B, and there is no hard evidence to show whether they were used or not.

As it was over 3ft longer than the Medium B, it proved possible to equip the Medium C with the full six-cylinder Ricardo engine. However, now that wartime restrictions on the use of alloys were coming to an end, it was possible to use more aluminium in the construction of the engine, so that it was appreciably lighter than the version adopted for the Mark V, although it still delivered the full 150hp. The engine was installed facing backwards so that it drove forwards through the clutch to a Wrigley four-speed gearbox, via a bevel box to cross shafts that engaged with epicyclic steering gears in the frames and then through two successive loops of chain and intermediate

His Majesty King George V and Queen Mary, with a bevy of senior officers, are introduced to a Medium C tank belonging to 2nd Battalion, Tank Corps, at Aldershot. The tank was later put through its paces for the benefit of the royal visitors, climbing over an earth mound and knocking down a brick wall.

sprockets to the final drive track sprockets at the back. The four-speed gearbox was identified as the component most likely to give trouble. Above the gearbox was the radiator, set longitudinally and cooled by a pair of opposed fans on a drive shaft.

One very typical Tritton touch first seen on the Whippet was a central cluster of seven track rollers on each side covering the main weight-bearing point on the frames that were fitted with roller bearings and contributed to the Medium C tank's excellent top speed for its day of nearly 8mph. Even so, the new Medium C was not quite so well armoured as Wilson's design, since maximum armour thickness was just 12mm covering vital parts compared with 14mm on the Medium B.

As with the Medium B, it was proposed to arm some if not all of the tanks with a new 2-pdr weapon, although whether this would have made it a male tank is not entirely clear (this term was never used with the medium tanks so it may have been considered as a means of enhancing the firepower of all tanks). In the event, as we have seen, production of the 2-pdr was halted because it compromised the 6-pdr programme.

However, there were proposals to create what was in effect a male version of the Medium C, referred to by the surprisingly modern term of 'tank destroyer'. No example was ever built that we know of, although drawings survive in the Illustrated Parts List so we have a pretty good idea of what it might have looked like. The superstructure was raised above the crew compartment, and a complete mounting for a 6-pdr gun provided in such a way that the weapon extended forwards above the driver's head. The original scheme seems to have been to use the 23-calibre weapon as fitted to Marks IV and V tanks[1], but upon consideration it was felt that the muzzle blast from this could affect the driver, so the plan was altered in favour of the old 40-calibre gun as fitted to male versions of the Mark I tank of 1916[2], which moved the muzzle a further 38in (96.9cm) away from the driver's position and presumably spared him from the effects of the blast. Since the 40-calibre gun had a marginally better

A Medium C on a road run just outside Bovington Camp. It has halted for this rather atmospheric photograph and one of the crew is posing on the side. A number of Medium C tanks were retained at Bovington, in addition to those serving with 2nd Battalion at Aldershot, and they were sent on some extensive road runs.

Medium C tanks took part in what we now know as the Royal Tournament in 1919. Here they are seen with their crews, relaxing between performances. They gave their display in conjunction with some Mark V** heavy tanks, including at least one mechanical bridgelayer.

1   See New Vanguard 133: *British Mark IV Tank* (Osprey, 2007) and New Vanguard 178: *Mark V Tank* (Osprey, 2011).

2   See New Vanguard 100: *British Mark I Tank 1916* (Osprey, 2004).

A Medium C tank on parade at Rugeley in Staffordshire at the end of the war. What it was doing there and where it had come from is unknown. Notice the open, double-flap roof hatch located ahead of the commander's cupola, and the partly open driver's visor.

performance than the later version in terms of range and muzzle velocity, this might have improved its performance against other tanks, but since it was never built or used in action this is only academic speculation. The drawings of the superstructure of the 6-pdr also show extensions bulging out over the tracks at each side, and it seems as if the side mountings for the Hotchkiss machine guns were moved here and set facing forwards.

Four Medium C tanks represented the Tank Corps at the London Victory Parade of July 1919. None ever went abroad, but a few were used at home in support of the civil powers at times of industrial unrest, such as the Liverpool police strike or the potential riots in Glasgow. Experience soon showed that armoured cars were far more suitable for this work, being more mobile and less threatening, but such was the reputation of tanks at this time they were chosen instead.

Twenty-four Medium C tanks formed A and B Companies of 2nd Battalion Tank Corps (12 tanks per company), which moved from Bovington to Farnborough in 1921 and became a common sight on the roads around that part of Surrey. They took part in a number of Southern Command exercises until replaced by more modern medium tanks from about 1923.

No Medium C survived to be preserved, but some six tanks were still around in 1930. They were taken out of store and sent to the Mechanical Warfare Experimental Establishment (MWEE) at Farnborough for potential use as tank recovery vehicles. Nothing survives to show what modifications might have been involved. In any case the project was abandoned, and with that the Medium C disappears from history.

The Victory Parade passing over Westminster Bridge on 19 July 1919. This picture shows the Tank Corps detachment of four Medium C tanks, preceded by a marching squad of officers and men representing the wartime Tank Corps. Two Tank Corps officers, Brigadier Hugh Elles and Colonel J. F. C. Fuller, led the procession on horseback.

MEDIUM D

Major Philip Johnson, who commanded No. 3 Advanced Workshops in France, was a gifted and inventive engineer who before the war had worked for Fowlers of Leeds in their Bombay office. Johnson's inventive genius was such that No. 3 Advanced Workshops was dedicated entirely to experimental work that they continued to do under Johnson's instructions when he was transferred to Tank Corps headquarters in France. Johnson was dedicated to making tanks go faster, and he realized that, in order to do this, tanks required springs. His first attempt to do this involved a Mark IV, although no details of this and no photograph have yet been found. Johnson then conducted a more radical experiment on a Medium A, which did achieve impressive results.

A full-size wooden mock-up of the Medium D showing the unusual layout, which condemned it in the eyes of many 'experts'. In fact, it was only ever meant to be a test bed for some revolutionary ideas. For some reason the mock-up was fitted with real weapons and mountings.

He did, however, also appreciate that providing springs for every wheel station increased the weight, and in an effort to overcome this developed a novel arrangement whereby a system of flexible steel wire rope was employed as the main suspension system, running over and under pulleys and connected to a spring at the end. Thus as each wheel rose over an obstacle it forced up the cable, which pulled on the spring. Once the tank was on a flat surface again, the spring and cable forced the suspension to level out. Johnson also came up with the idea of threading the track shoes onto a loop of wire rope that ran around the suspension. This caused the track to bend around the curve as the tank steered, reducing the side thrust on a conventional machine and making steering easier. These ideas were first tried on a modified Mark V heavy tank, and then applied to a new tank of Johnson's own design. This was the Medium D. It was such a revolutionary design that an officer from Tank Corps HQ in France, Major Giffard Le Q. Martel, came over to Britain to inspect the full-size wooden mock-up.

Even when it first appeared, it seems obvious that nobody was ever likely to mistake the new tank for anything else. It was very distinctive. The crew

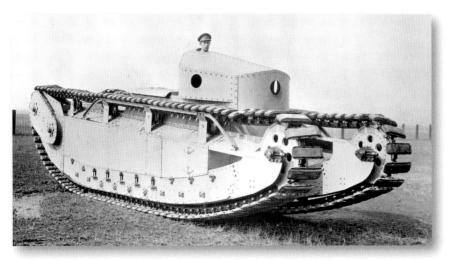

An original Medium D tank before being fitted with weapons mounts or a head cover for the driver. This photograph emphasizes how narrow it was, which is why it was reckoned to be unstable in the water. It has, however, a very striking appearance when compared with wartime tanks.

One of the original Medium D tanks that Philip Johnson took out to India. It is clad in panels of asbestos in an effort to reduce the heat. It was also suggested that the tank should be sprayed with water to keep the heat down, but nobody explained where the water was supposed to come from.

compartment at the front was essentially oval in plan form with mountings for three Hotchkiss machine guns, one at the front and one each side. Above and behind them sat the driver, for whom a cupola was provided, although there was no similar facility for a commander unless this duty devolved upon the driver; however, as Johnson was at pains to point out to his critics, the tank was really no more than a mechanical test bed and other matters could be attended to once these basic problems had been solved. Another curious feature that an observer would note is that the rear drive sprocket was set rather higher than the idler. This was a typical Johnson feature and said to be arranged so that the tank could tackle a difficult obstacle in reverse.

G

1: MEDIUM D

Looking unlike any tank ever seen before, the Medium D and its derivatives were a revolutionary step in tank design. Designed by Lt-Col Philip Johnson and built by Wolseley Motors Ltd of Birmingham, a Vickers subsidiary, and powered by a six-cylinder Siddeley Puma aero engine, the Medium D was fast for its time but not always reliable. A crew of four occupied the structure at the front; the driver sitting above and behind them, although at this stage his armoured head cover has not been fitted. The wire rope suspension is hidden by the track frames; note that these are higher at the back than the front. The tracks can however be seen, narrow steel shoes with wooden inserts threaded onto a wire rope core.

Johnson never regarded the Medium D as a finished tank design, only as a testbed to try out the experimental suspension and tracks. Most of these tanks were soon scrapped although one remained for some years as an exhibit in the original, open-air Tank Museum at Bovington. It was ultimately broken up and none survive today.

2: STUDEBAKER LIGHT TANK

Although not directly connected with the Medium A the Studebaker tank was probably considered as a successor. It was designed by two British officers attached to the British Tank Mission in Washington DC, who had already been offered a number of 110hp Hall Scott aero engines which they thought would suit a light tank. The Studebaker Corporation of South Bend, Indiana, was already well known as a carmaker and had become involved in the production of a small and simple supply tractor, based on the British Newton Tractor and produced on behalf of Sir Percival Perry, head of the British Tank Mission. The new tank would use the tracks and running gear of this tractor.

A photograph of the tank outside the Studebaker Factory shows it with two small machine-gun turrets on top but these appear to have been removed by the time the tank arrived in Britain. It was photographed in this form a number of times but there are no surviving accounts of any trials and one suspects that with the end of the war it was quietly done away with.

1

2

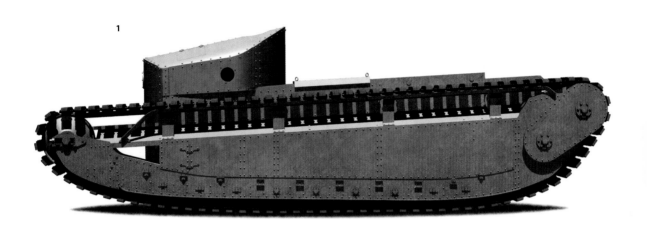

The Medium D* ('Medium D star'), which was photographed in the original open air Tank Museum at Bovington. What looks like an extension of the cab is in fact part of a Medium C tank parked alongside. Although it was wider than the Medium D, this is not obvious from the photograph.

The Medium D was powered by a 240hp Siddeley Puma aircraft engine, a water-cooled straight six. The transmission, upon which Walter Wilson was consulted, involved three-speed epicyclics on each output shaft that provided gear changing and graduated steering facilities. These controls are all said to have been hydraulic. Every effort was made to keep the weight down in the interests of speed and because, in line with Johnson's creed, the tank was intended to be amphibious. Armour was therefore limited to 10mm around the crew and 6mm elsewhere, resulting in an all-up weight of 13½ tons. Tests conducted by the Admiralty at Johnson's request suggested that the long, narrow tank would be unstable in the water.

The Medium D** ('Medium D two star') afloat in the river at Christchurch during an amphibious trial. Walking along the tracks is not recommended; they were used to drive it along in the water. This version was both wider and longer than the original, which is why it floated a lot better.

All told, ten prototypes were ordered: four from Fowlers of Leeds (two of which were never completed) and six from Vickers through their Wolseley subsidiary in Birmingham. Of these one was apparently destroyed by fire at Christchurch, two were sent out for trials in India, and two more were completed as improved models. The fate of the others is not recorded.

The Medium D* looked very similar to the Medium D, although in fact it was wider, at 8ft 5ins instead of 7ft 3ins, to improve stability in the water. However, it was still not good enough to satisfy the Admiralty. It is also reported to have had four-speed epicyclics in the transmission, all of which increased the weight by one ton. Its service career is not recorded, although it ended its days in the open-air Tank Museum at Bovington.

To some extent the Medium D** could be regarded as a completely new tank, although it was assembled from parts intended for a cancelled Medium D. To begin with, it had been widened to 9ft, which at last ensured that it was stable in the water, and was nearly 2ft longer. It was powered by a high compression version of the Siddeley Puma, which delivered 300hp, and the transmission involved a primary four-speed and reverse gearbox with experimental Rackham clutches on the output shafts for steering. Weight had now increased to 15 tons. In 1921 it was sent for conversion, and when it emerged again it was equipped with a 370hp Rolls-Royce engine and a Williams-Janney hydraulic steering system and final drive, which had already failed in other tank trials. It does not appear to have done any better

The Medium DM (or D Modified) tank, probably photographed at Farnborough. The number 2 on the front was the number issued by the Tank Testing Section. This tank featured two cupolas, one for the commander and one for the driver, each of which seems to have obscured the view of the other.

this time, being recorded as ceasing running in August 1922 and as being broken up about three years later.

The final manifestation of the Medium D appeared in the form of the Medium D Modified (or Medium DM), two of which were delivered by the Ordnance Factory at Woolwich in August 1921. Johnson by this time had been appointed head of the Department of Tank Design and Experiment, located at Charlton Park near Woolwich. Both tanks were powered by a 260hp Rolls-Royce Eagle V12. Although it is claimed that each tank had a different transmission for trial purposes, neither type is specified.

One feature that Johnson may have introduced to satisfy his critics was a second cupola, presumably for the tank commander, situated alongside that provided for the driver. The Medium DM was also amphibious, although one of them sank in the river Thames and had to be fished out. Both tanks were sent to the new Tank Testing Section at Farnborough in August 1921, where they are recorded as ceased running a year later and subsequently broken up.

Although this ended the medium tank saga, it should be noted that Johnson persisted in designing and building prototypes for a year or so in the face of increasing financial stringency before his department was closed down and the project dropped.

The Medium D was visualized by the Tank Corps' tactical eminence J. F. C. Fuller as the epitome of his war-winning Plan 1919, and he clung to this despite mounting evidence of its unreliability. Indeed at one point while in the War Office Fuller records that in pursuit of the ideal tank for Plan 1919 he was torn between increasing the supply of Medium C tanks or investing the available funds in the unproven potential of the Medium D. He decided in favour of thelatter, and was spared embarrassment only by the ending of World War I.

THE STUDEBAKER TANK

Although it was essentially a light tank, the Studebaker tank was clearly intended as a rival to the Medium D, and as such deserves a place here. In the summer of 1918, staff at the British Tank Mission in Washington were offered a quantity of Hall Scott four-cylinder, water-cooled aero engines rated at 110hp, which they believed would also be suitable for tanks. As a result, two British officers serving with the mission came up with the design of a light tank and asked the Studebaker Corporation of South Bend, Indiana to produce a prototype.

Among those involved with the Tank Mission in Washington was Sir Percival Perry (knighted 1917), who before the war had managed production for the Ford Company in England and built it up to be a highly popular brand. A factory had been established at Trafford Park, Manchester in 1911, which was taken over by the government in 1914 and Perry became deputy to Vice-Admiral Moore at the Mechanical Warfare Department. By 1918 Perry was operating out of Washington in charge of production of a very basic tracked load carrier for the British Army, known as the Newton Tractor in Britain after its inventor Colonel Henry Newton. The plan was to take advantage of American production capacity and manufacture large numbers in the United States.

Orders were placed for 10,000 machines with Buick and 5,000 each with Willys-Overland and Studebaker. The tank was to be based upon the same

technology, albeit with a fully armoured body and a much more powerful engine. Perry's involvement in the design of the tank is not entirely clear, although a sentence in the *History of the Ministry of Munitions* states 'Sir Percival Perry left for the United States on 31 August 1918, and part of the work undertaken in his American offices was the development of an experimental fighting tank designed to use the 110hp Hall-Scott engine as a power unit'. A photograph taken outside the Studebaker plant shows the tank with two small machine-gun turrets, one behind the other, on top of the superstructure. (See Plate G2).

The tank was certainly completed and shipped to Britain, but details are few. It is credited with a top speed of 12mph and presumably required a minimum crew of three, but no other technical details survive. Photographs of it in Britain appear to show that the two turrets had been removed, but whether it was tested and rejected, or the premature end of the war caused the order to be cancelled, is not known.

The Studebaker tank photographed in Britain, now without its two machine-gun turrets. For some reason the photographer elected to take photographs of it from a very low angle, which over-emphasized its size. In reality it was quite a small tank. Compare this picture with the drawing (Plate G2) of the tank in its original form.

INDEX